Acknowledgements

I would like to take the opportunity to thank the people who have come alongside me while writing this study guide. First and foremost, my friend and sister in Christ, Bonnie Dye, and my granddaughter, Revae Mitchell, for helping edit this guide and for giving me such great feedback. I want to also thank Sherry Anderson, author and Florida state leader of Aglow ministries, who really encouraged me to go deeper in my study guide. Because of her encouragement I revised this study guide.

Thank you all so much for your help and support.

I am very excited about the opportunity to offer this study to go along with my book, New Beginnings.

My hope is that the study guide will take each reader into a deeper walk with God and answer questions regarding God's character, who the Holy Spirit is, and why knowing Him is so important. God wants you to know Him, and He sent His one and only Son, Jesus, to bridge the gap between heaven and Earth for you to find Him. May you always know true freedom that is only found in Christ. It's for freedom that Christ set us free. Galatians 5:1

I have added a tool in this study guide to help you learn not only how to memorize scripture but also how to get scripture into you. God's word is not only timeless but a powerful way to guide us in this sometimes times troubled life.

Thank you all so much for your help and support.

Terri Leonard

Contents

Week 1: What does it mean to be born again? 3

Week 2: Who is God? 13

Week 3: Why the Holy Spirit? 27

Week 4: How do I follow Jesus? And how do I have a Jesus Culture? 37

Week 5: Who is the church? 53

Directions for Three Question Bible Study for Scripture Memorization

STEP 1: WHAT VERSE(S) DO I WANT TO MEMORIZE?

The first step is to write out the Bible verse(s) you have chosen in its entirety on the Bible study sheet. When you have finished writing the scripture, move on to step 2. Every day, re-read the complete verse.

STEP 2: WHAT DOES GOD'S WORD SAY?

After reading the verse, make a phrase-by-phrase list of the verse you are memorizing. You should only memorize one phrase each day. Take more days if needed! Never rush. When you make your list, do not paraphrase the text but use actual words from the scripture. Ask yourself the following questions:

• Who is speaking? • What is the subject? • Where is it taking place? • When did it happen?

STEP 3: WHAT DOES GOD'S WORD MEAN?

Learn the lessons. After reading the phrase, look for a lesson to learn. Ask yourself the following questions:

• What can I learn from what is taking place or what is being said? • What are the people in the passage doing that I should be doing? • Is there a command I should obey? • Is there a promise I should make? • Is there a warning I should heed? • Is there an example I should follow?

Focus on spiritual lessons.

STEP 4: WHAT IS GOD'S WORD SAYING TO YOU?

Listen to His voice. Although this step will be the most meaningful for you, you can't do it effectively until you complete the first three steps. Listen for God to speak to you through His Word. Remember not to rush this process. It may take you several moments of prayerful meditation to discover meaningful lessons from the phrase you are reading and hear God speaking to you. The object is not to "get through it" but to develop your personal relationship with God.

STEP 5: HOW WILL I APPLY GOD'S WORD TO MY DAILY LIFE?

Live it out! Read your chosen Scripture prayerfully and thoughtfully as you listen for God to speak. When He does, record what it is that God seems to be saying to you and your response to Him.

STEP 6: PRAY AND RESPOND

Write out your prayer to God, thanking Him for His Word.

Modified from Ann Graham Lotz the Daniel Prayer Bible Study.

What does it mean to be born again?

Week 1

Scripture of Focus - Galatians 3:26

"For you are all sons of God through faith in Christ Jesus."

Read the following pages of New Beginning:

Understanding the language of faith - Page 1

Coming Home – Page 15

Forgiveness – Page 13

Meditate on scripture and reading.

The Language of Faith:

The way we experience God's grace and mercy is very individual and personal. For some, it feels like a sudden revelation, while for others, it takes time to walk through a process of acceptance.

Perhaps for you, it felt as though you turned a corner in your life and discovered God was already right in front of you, or maybe you felt like He chased you down and caught you from behind.

Regardless of how you might describe your own journey, all such stories share a few things in common: a change in what you believe, a transfer of loyalty, and a reversal in the direction from which you were traveling. God forgives, saves, restores, and reconciles us back to him.

I don't want to assume everyone reading this is already a follower of Christ. If by chance you are not. But you're searching.

Know that God has a destiny and purpose for your life. He sent His only Son, who willingly gave His life for us. He came to a planet of orphans to make us His family and rescue us.

You need to surrender your life to Jesus and ask Him to come and change you. Ask Him to forgive you of your sins. Ask Him to heal your heart. Decide to turn from your old life and walk on a new path with Him.

If you have said this prayer, please send me a message. My contact info is in the book that accompanies this workbook.

Know that you are loved just as you are, but He loved you too much to keep you there. **God is our New Beginning!**

Coming Home:

The story of the prodigal son follows the journey of a man who strays far from home and even farther from the man he is destined to be. You can read it in Luke 15:11-32. He trusts the character of his father. Consequently, he backs away from his broken and hopeless life, turns around, and walks back home.

That is what repentance is**. It is a homecoming.** And when we return home, we do not find a Father who is angry or ready to say, "I told you so." Rather, we see a Father who runs towards us with loving arms. Jesus does not call us to repentance to simply change our behavior. It is about so much more. It is about whom our trust is placed.

Describe the perfect homecoming. What would it look like? When you made the choice to go back home, what reaction would you expect?

Do yourself a favor and forgive:

Becoming a Christian is not about what you do for God; it's about what God has already done for you. Jesus paid our debt, freed us from sin and death, and reconciled us to God, our Father, and others. Jesus divinely disrupted and reversed the story of humanity. Forgiveness is a fundamental aspect of our faith, and its significance cannot be overstated. It's not only crucial to God but also for our own well-being and spiritual growth.

Forgiveness – Jesus paid a debt He did not owe, and we could not pay, so that the charges of sin against us are canceled. Through Jesus, we experience forgiveness and cleansing. Grace and forgiveness are intertwined together. "It's by Grace we are saved."

"He made the One who did not know sin to be sin for us so that we might become the righteousness of God in Him." (2 Corinthians 5:21)

Where do you feel in your life it's hard to forgive? Yourself? Others? Are you ready to let go and allow The Holy Spirit to exchange the pain with His healing and grace?

Because we live in a fallen world, we face the reality that there will be a time of being hurt, and if you're not careful, it will lead to offense. After an offense comes, unforgiveness and offense can be like an arrow dipped in poison. If allowed, the offense can bring bitterness, which can filter deep into our hearts. We, perhaps, unknowingly, begin to hold onto unforgiveness. This can affect our thoughts and even paralyze us and affect how we live and love.

The Bait of Satan Is Offense:

Unforgiveness holds us hostage. When Jesus was betrayed by Judas, He did not allow the pain of the moment to keep him from the purposes of His future. Unforgiveness can keep you from your destiny in the kingdom.

It takes three to reconcile. You- the offender – and God.

What is forgiveness?

We need to first start with what it isn't. It is not minimizing what has happened to you. The Father's heart was broken for you. Don't just shrug it off or say... It doesn't matter. It does matter, and you matter.

You must take some time to unpack this and ask the comforter, who is the Holy Spirit, to help you release it to the Father so that you can then release the one/ones who hurt you. I am not saying for a moment that what happened was right or fair.

I am saying, for your sake, you must release them.

If you don't, it will stay with you. It will rob you of your God-given freedom.

Thousands of years ago, the Romans worked very hard to come up with the cruelest tortures imaginable. One such torture was when you were found guilty of murder. They would tie the dead body to you.

Every waking hour, you had to carry this dead body attached to you. As the body decomposes, the toxins are released into your body and slowly and painfully kill you. Holding a grudge against someone and refusing to forgive will slowly poison your heart.

Forgiveness doesn't mean reconciliation:

Reconciliation and forgiveness are two different things. It takes three to reconcile. You- the offender – and God. But you certainly don't have to have reconciliation to forgive. You must do this even if they're not sorry. Forgiveness is for you.

It is easy to make reconciliation a preface before forgiveness. I remember when someone very close to me hurt me deeply. I said in my heart, "I'll forgive them as soon as they apologize." What I did was make myself a hostage to the one who had hurt me.

Reconciliation must be done by both parties. One doesn't always lead to the other. They must sincerely apologize to you first before they have the right to your trust again. Forgiveness is a spiritual act; this means you are relying on God's grace to be able to forgive. Our capacity to forgive does not depend on anyone else's behavior or permission. Reconciliation isn't required for forgiveness.

Repentance: This means to turn away from doing the wrong thing and go in a different direction.

Making Restitution: Doing whatever you can to make things right.

Rebuilding Your Trust: They need to show themselves to be changed in action and words.

Forgiveness is a gift! Free to give and to receive. Unforgiveness keeps us held hostage to a person or event like a prisoner until we release them to God. When we do, the Holy Spirit comes into this area and brings peace and freedom. God is faithful to help us with this if we ask Him to give us the grace and strength and the **want to**… forgive. Choosing not to forgive gets us stuck in our own past, preventing us from moving forward. Without forgiveness, you are constantly stuck in your own past. Many people waste <u>years</u> of their lives in bitterness and resentment when they could, through forgiveness, have lived that time in joy. Read Page 35 in <u>New Beginnings</u> on inner healing.

God's desire is for you to have a whole and healed heart. To walk in your truest identity without believing lies about yourself. When we forgive, we are set free from the unholy alliance with the enemy. If we live our life with unhealed wounds, the enemy attaches a lie or lies to each wound about ourselves that can cause us to believe lies about ourselves, such as I am not very smart… I will never get ahead… No one cares about me. Does any of this sound familiar?

These unhealed wounds can cause us to be easily offended or feel rejected… when it may not even be true. When we have unhealed pain in our hearts, it is like a little place in our soul that is broken and crushed. When we forgive, it often brings healing to our bodies. Even scientists realize when someone is holding on to unforgiveness, whether it's for someone or even unforgiveness for themselves, it can harbor diseases and pain. **Jesus proclaims over us that He will heal the brokenhearted and set the captives free.**

<u>*Read Matthew 18:21-35*</u> *The parable of the unforgiving servant*

"Then Peter came to Jesus and asked, "Lord, how many times shall I forgive my brother or sister who sins against me? Up to seven times?" Jesus answered, "I tell you, not seven times, but seventy-seven times. In other words, an unlimited time. Jesus then told a parable of a servant who owed in today's market over a billion dollars.

The King was going to throw him in debtors' prison. The servant fell to his knees and begged for forgiveness. The King had compassion and forgave him for his extravagant debt. Now, the servant went and found a man who owed him a few thousand dollars.

The man begged for mercy, and the King's servant had zero compassion and had him thrown in prison!

Several of the King's servants saw this go down and were deeply grieved and told the King. He immediately summoned him. The King told the wicked servant how could you not have compassion and mercy when I extended compassion and mercy unto you? Take this ungrateful servant where there is deep darkness, wailing, and torment!

The takeaway Jesus wanted Peter to get was to let your mercy have no limits. Matthew states it clearly… A person who does not forgive others will not be forgiven by God. Forgiving is not optional in the kingdom of God; it is mandatory.

The overarching message here is that if we refuse to forgive, **we have forgotten how much we have been forgiven for**. God, without hesitation, the moment we ask Him for forgiveness, not only forgives us but never remembers it again. Remembering that God's forgiveness of our sins should inspire us to forgive others should become our perspective. It reminds us of the immense grace we have received and should extend to others. So, whether you're a new Christian or you have walked with the Lord for many years, this is a lifestyle and a continuous practice that we should carry, and daily ask God to search our hearts to illuminate it for us.

That is how we must with gratitude and awareness of how much we have been forgiven to be able to forgive others.

Ephesians 4:32: "Be kind and compassionate to one another, forgiving each other just as in Christ God has forgiven you. The Bible is very clear. If we don't forgive… We will not be forgiven. Unforgiveness keeps the pain alive. Unforgiveness never lets the wound heal. You risk going through life being reminded of what was done to you. Stirring up that pain can make you progressively angrier. Which keeps you in the trap that Satan will trap you with. being offended.

"He is so rich in kindness and grace that He purchased our freedom with the blood of His Son and forgave our sins." Ephesians 1:7

3 Question Bible Study Work Sheet

Read God's Word

Galatians 3:26

For you are all sons of God through faith in Christ Jesus.

1: What Does God's Word Say? List the facts	*2:* What Does God's Word Means? List the lessons	*3:* What Does God's Word Mean in My Life? Listen to His voice
Phrase 1 - Phrase 2 -		

Phrase 3 –		

Pray and Respond:

Write out your prayer.

Live It Out:

How will I apply this to my daily life?

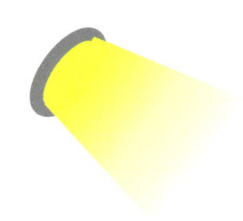

Who is God?

Week 2

Focus Scripture: Exodus 34:6

And He passed in front of Moses, Proclaiming, "The Lord, the Lord, the compassionate and gracious God, slow to anger, abounding in love and faithfulness."

Read the following pages of <u>New Beginnings:</u>

- Seeing the Big Picture – Page 3
- Jesus, Fully Man and Fully God – Page 11
- The Nature and Character of God – Page 59

Meditate on scripture and reading.

God, who is 'compassionate and gracious' as our memory verse says, wants us to live our lives in true freedom.

Living your life in freedom:

I just finished a wonderful curriculum called <u>Freedom</u> from Highlands Church. The first part is very foundational to what I wanted to cover here. I'm sharing some of what I learned with you. I hope you look up this important study on YouTube. They also have study guides available on Amazon.

A big part of living our life in freedom is to know the difference between living your life in the Tree of Life. Not in the tree of the knowledge of good and evil.

I'll start with a story.

There was a pastor at a local coffee shop working on his sermon. A rough-looking guy with tattoos everywhere and pink hair saw the Bible and said, "I hate religious people."

The pastor quickly responded, "Jesus hates religion, too." The guy ordered his coffee, sat next to the pastor, and asked, "What do you mean Jesus hates religion too?" He said, "I know what kind of Christians you're talking about. I know the kind of Christians you have been exposed to, and unfortunately, Christianity has a branding problem. Jesus blasted the religious people called Pharisees (they were the strict religious people of Jesus's day). He called them 'whitewashed tombs for looking beautiful on the outside and full of dead people's bones on the inside. For appearing *righteous but being full of hypocrisy and lawlessness. Matthew 23:27-28*

There are two approaches to God I'm going to discuss, but many have been exposed to the wrong approach. It may look right, but it is not. You see, true Christianity isn't really about a denomination or a religion or an organization. It's about a relationship with Jesus and knowing him, not about just being a part of a denomination.

The man had a vape pen and said, "What do you think your God would say about this… I love to get my drink on!"

There are two approaches to God I'm going to discuss, but many have been exposed to the wrong approach. It may look right, but it is not. You see, true Christianity isn't really about a denomination or a religion or an organization. It's about a relationship with Jesus and knowing him, not about just being a part of a denomination.

The man had a vape pen and said, "What do you think your God would say about this… I love to get my drink on!"

The pastor, to prove his point, said, "I don't think he cares about that. I think he cares about you. And he would talk to you about that later."

It's important that you understand you must have the right approach to God. One is through work/performance, and the other is through trust/grace. The correct approach is so important. What is your motivation, and what is going on inside is critical to the process.

This approach came in the 2nd story of the Garden of Eden. We have a choice of how we are going to live our life out for God and what approach we are going to take. The first story was about creation. By the way, that is the first story of our life too, you were born. The 2nd story is about your life too. You have a choice in how you will view God and how you will approach Him as well.

THE CHOICE was given to Adam and Eve. God said, *"You can eat from any tree, but you cannot eat from the tree of the knowledge of good and evil."* God said when you do, you shall surely die. He wasn't talking about a physical death but a spiritual death. A death to your dreams is a death to your marriage. Genisis 2:16&17

Satan was using even what seemed like something good to Eve to deceive her. When you eat of this tree, you will be more like God. Sometimes, it even seems good what you're pursuing, but if you pay attention to the fruit coming from it, you can see it's from the wrong tree. Studying the word of God is important, but if your approach is to do this, you can, hopefully, please God. Be careful because He loves you no matter what. It can become works not out of love for Him to find Him in the scriptures.

The Tree of the Knowledge of Good and evil says you must work to get to God. This comes from a knowledge base instead of a transformational base. John 5:39 Jesus said, "*You study scripture because you think that in them you have eternal life. These are the very scriptures that testify about me, yet you refuse to come to me to have life."* The goal isn't how many chapters… but did you find me in the chapters?

When we choose to be independent and live in the tree of the knowledge of good and evil, we do things on our own in our own strength. This leads to a life of work and performance.

Every day, we have a choice of law or grace or a Life of separation from God. You can't miss this… It's determined by our approach to God.

When we choose to live from the tree of life, it is a heart relationship with God. We receive the fact that the price for your salvation has already been paid. This is something that can be applied to all areas of your life. *"I love Him because He first loved me."* It's about relationships and a transformed heart. The Tree of Life is more than a bible story. It can be your way of life.

Tree of Life:

Freedom, Grace, God is good, God is forgiving, God is trustworthy.

Tree of the knowledge of good and evil:

This leads to bondage, The law and works lead to spiritual death, God is judgmental, and we are condemned. Keep trying to get God's approval.

Satan tempts Adam and Eve, and they fall. When Satan told them that the fruit would help her gain wisdom, she believed it would help her be more like God. The problem is having knowledge about God is different than having God inside of you. It's important to note that Satan cannot force us to do anything. We must believe what he is saying first, and that gives him the permission he needs to ensnare you with his lies.

Shame causing them to hide from God is now introduced into the story. But don't miss the part of the story where God came looking for them. God cannot be in the presence of sin. Sin, on our part, separates us from Him. But God always pursues us with His goal. Relationship. Jesus came to seek and save the lost and reconcile them back to Father God.

The Tree of Life brings freedom and grace and leads us to eternal life. God is good, and God is forgiving, but that doesn't give us the 'go ahead' to do what we want. Because God is also holy, Paul said in Romans 6:2, *"So shall we continue to sin that grace may abound?* Paul replies with a resounding, God Forbid." To desire to sin shows a misunderstanding of this abundant grace and contempt for Jesus's sacrifice. Either we believe what God says is true or not.

As stated at the beginning of this discussion, it's about our approach to God that matters. Living in the tree of the knowledge of good and evil shows up as condemnation, selfishness, jealousy, unforgiveness, strife, and bondages in your life. Living in the Tree of Life shows up as good fruit: life, grace, joy, peace, acceptance, love, generosity, kindness, and unity.

You have a choice in how you approach God and how you're going to live your life, whether you're in the fruit of the tree of the knowledge of good and evil. Stop, and take some time to reflect with God. Ask the Holy Spirit what's really going on and get out of agreement with it, repent, and go in a different direction!

God is always right, with arms open wide to help guide you to the right path. The path that always leads to peace. This can be difficult to see for those who have the wrong view of God if you think of God as this distant approach. You will approach Him as a harsh God. Again, the tree of the knowledge of good and evil says... be careful. He's not in a good mood; he's mad and easy to anger... just like your dad was.

Now, I could go on a rabbit trail right now with what I just said when I realized that my relationship with my earthly parents greatly impacted my view of God. This really opened my eyes as I pursued inner healing. I saw God as harsh and distant, just like my dad. I didn't realize until I pursued inner healing how much it affected my approach to my heavenly Father.

As you progress in your walk with God and through this study guide, you will be able to use the Tree of Life thinking as a framework for the way you approach any situation you encounter in your daily life. It is so important to get to know your Bible and read it daily. It will help you build strong muscles that need to be strengthened. Different ones that you're not used to using. As a follower of Jesus, we build our faith muscles through our time with the Word and the times we spend with Jesus. Learning to hear His voice. Retraining our thought process to line up with God's truth. And just like with weight training, you need a spotter. A friend and a small group will help you in this faith-building process. To help encourage you and even challenge you when needed. Living in the Tree of Life results in having true fellowship with God and others.

John 17:3 says, *"Now this eternal life: that they know you, the only true God, and Jesus Christ, whom you have sent."* To know means in the Greek to recognize, to understand, or to understand completely. This indicates a relationship. The only way to really have this promised abundant life is to truly know this amazing, loving God.

God desired a relationship with us from the beginning of creation. Ephesians 1:7,8 We are sons and daughter's no longer servants because He sees us already wrapped up in Christ. In the same way, God loves His precious Son, who sacrificed His life for us. God loves us the same way.

Wow, that is amazing right there. The same love the Father has for His Son... He has for us!

If we really believe that we are that loved, it will totally change our approach and our view of God. Imagine that kind of perspective? When you know how much you are already loved, it will keep you living from the tree of the knowledge of good and evil. You will not want to sin, to have one foot in the world and one foot in the church, as they say.

Why? Because you know and are confident in the fact you are so loved, and you don't want to displease the father. Paul said it well when he told the church of Ephesus that his prayer for them was *that they be rooted and grounded in love and that they may have the strength to comprehend with all the saints what is the breadth and length and height and depth, to know the love of Christ that surpasses all understanding. Ephesians 3:17-19*

Now, that is living in the Tree of Life with a heavenly Father who is always good. And is always there for you and me.

God is Always Good, Never Bad, and Never Both

Basic Christianity 101:

The most important things - basic doctrine:

- Hear the message of Jesus.
- Accept the message by faith.
- Receive salvation.
- Receive the Holy Spirit.
- Pray for the sick and those in need.
- Share our faith with others.
- Disciple new believers.

After salvation, we begin building our relationship with God the Father, Christ the Son, and the Holy Spirit. The stronger this relationship becomes, the truer our image of the character of God becomes. As we grow, our identity is in who He is rather than the false conceptions placed in our hearts by the world. The world is fractured by sin, bringing hurt, pain, and wounds to our hearts, which distort our perception of who God is.

The Gospel is truth. Our Heavenly Father is love and loves us. We are in Christ, and Christ is in us. We are being transformed into His image and His purpose for our lives. This takes time. It is a process.

Having the right perspective on the real image of the one true God is the new beginning. In life, what people perceive of us, right or wrong, determines how they think and act toward us. It is the same with the image we have of God. The image we have of God can make or break us in spiritual matters because it affects how we approach Him. Our personal, collective knowledge of God is what forms His image in our minds. If that knowledge is not sound, our image of Him is blurry. A blurry and distorted image of God will confuse our relationship with Him. It will weaken our faith, hinder our prayers, and even interfere with finding God's perfect will and purpose for our lives.

Why do people have a wrong perception of God? Either they do not know the Bible, so their spiritual opinions are based on personal perceptions, or they rely on the spiritual 'opinions' of others. Without a Biblical foundation, people do not realize the astounding contrast between the Old Testament and the New Testament. The difference between the old covenant and the new covenant. The Bible tells us in Romans 8 that Christ accomplished what the law was powerless to do because it was weakened by the flesh, sin. It is the difference between living under the law and living by grace.

God's true nature is not defined by our personal opinions. We are not God; therefore, we do not get to "make" Him in our image. The only set of character truths that define Him are those that He has revealed to us in His Word. When we do not know His Word, we lack spiritual facts and have opened the door for personal opinions and secular concepts to paint our picture of Him. These false truths have even invaded the church and have undermined the church's efforts to present a loving God to humanity.

When people believe the allegation that God is involved in their suffering, they frequently run *from* Him instead of *to* Him. Even believers, if they accept these subtle deceptions, find their hearts contaminated with a drop of uncertainty about God's goodness. That drop can damage their spiritual strength, distance their relationship with God, and ruin their prayers.

This is our anchor point: God's goodness. With it, we can always know where God stands on every issue and every event in our lives. It is this: God is a Good Father. He is a good, good father. The Bible says that God is even better than the best earthly parent. Matthew 7:7-11 says, "If you then being evil, know how to give good gifts to your children, how much more will your father who is in heaven give good things to those who ask Him."

There is a story of a Pastor whose father was told when he was young that his father died because God needs good people in Heaven, and that is why God took his father. Can you imagine how devastating that was for this thirteen-year-old young man to hear? Or when others hear things like, "God took your baby because he needed another angel in Heaven.". That is basically saying, "God is good, but" – there is *no* but. So, if God is good, why does He allow evil to exist? What a paradox! It has boggled the intellects of the greatest minds in history. But

God is God, isn't He? Yes, he is. And He is omnipotent and can do anything He chooses, right? Yes, He can. But what if one of God's choices was to partner with man rather than control him?

What do you think about the word "allow"? When challenged on it, most people admit that God wouldn't cause a bad thing. They want God to remain good. No matter how it is framed, the words "God allows" insinuate to many that God plays an active role in hardship. He may not have caused it, but he sure did allow it.

Does God allow evil to happen? In the most fundamental way, He does allow people the capacity to make bad choices. This comes from His desire to protect our free will because our free will is the very root of our humanity and individuality and the means by which we manifest the image of God. Free will has such a high value for God that Jesus died on the cross to preserve our ability to choose Him.

When we receive Christ, we enter a house with protective walls around it. The enemy can never remove those walls. We belong to Christ. In this house, there are many rooms, and God allows us to choose the rooms we enter. But… Unless we seek His guidance, we may go to rooms that are not the best for us to enter. When we choose the room rather than letting God direct us, there are consequences to our choices that God would not have chosen for us, but He allows because of our choices.

We must all always remember that God is not only love, but He is also just. Justice is something we desire, but you cannot have justice without judgment. While there are consequences for our choices and the choices of others, as believers, Christ has taken our judgment, and we are just before God. We live in a fallen world, but the battle has been won.

The Bible says there is one thing that God cannot do. He cannot lie. Titus 1:2: "God, who cannot lie, promised before time began…" God created the universe for the galaxy, the galaxy for the solar system, and the solar system for the Earth. He created the Earth for man. And when He put man in the Earth, He gave man the responsibility to govern it. (Refer back to The Garden in New Beginning, page 5.)

On page five, The Garden, it says everything God planted was beautiful. There was no death, only life. It was perfect and exactly the right size for two people to manage. When God put Adam and Eve in the garden, He gave them a job to work and keep the garden. He said to be fruitful and multiply. God said, "Subdue the earth," which is a military term that means conquer and control, for outside of this garden, there was chaos. Beyond the Garden of Eden is where the enemy, Satan, lived.

Genesis 1:26-28 "Then God said… Let them, man and woman, have dominion over… all the Earth." Dominion over all the Earth! The responsibility to govern gave mankind a say-so in allowing evil into this world system - or not. We shouldn't point the finger at God. The world was not supposed to have even one ounce of suffering in it. Suffering was not in the original blueprint for life. God created the Earth to be a perfect paradise where mankind would only know life, joy, and peace. But man was deceived and tempted by the lies of Satan, who desired to break man's perfect fellowship with God. Remember, the Bible tells us that God walked with Adam and Eve in the cool of the evening (Genesis 3:8), perfect fellowship as God designed it. But man…

God wanted us to have free will. A free will to choose Him or to choose something else. He gave us the responsibility to take care of this world. We brought suffering, pain, sin, and death into this world. God's will was never for death to have rule over us, ever! When we say that God allows rape, incest, murder, etc., we are basically saying God is 'bipolar'-both good and bad. God is only good, only kind, patient, longsuffering, and gentle. As your first memory verse states, His true nature and character will never change. It is critical that we understand this precept and have it as our foundation - God is always good, and He is light. Light will always dispel darkness. James 1:17 tells us that every good and perfect gift comes from God, who does not change like shifting shadows.

"Obviously, this [does God permit bad things to happen] is a very complicated issue, and there are no truly satisfying simple answers. However, this is my take on. As to Job, I like Bill Johnson's position that the book of Job is the question, and Jesus is the answer. If reading the book of Job doesn't lead you to Jesus, then you're reading it wrong.

The overarching message of the book of Job is not to teach a theology of God but to get you to quit putting God in a box! The only truly trustworthy theological statement in the book of Job is at the end when Job is face to face with God! Job repents for the audacity of trying to say he knows why God does what he does.

We live in a fallen world and in the midst of the consequences of humanity advocating its authority to the devil. Finally, Jesus is perfect theology. Hebrews chapter 1 tells us that He is the perfect, complete image of the Father. Jesus said if you have seen Me, you have seen the Father. What did Jesus do? According to Acts, He went around doing good and destroying all the works of the devil. What are the works of the devil? In John 10, Jesus tells us that the devil comes to kill, steal, and destroy. Jesus said that we might have life and have it more abundantly. What did that look like? Jesus healed ALL that came to him.

If Jesus was healing those who the Father afflicted by His same argument about the devil, He is divided against the Father's will, and the house will fall. He's a good Father. If I ascribe to the Heavenly Father something that I, as a human Father, would be jailed for if I did it to my daughter - then that is NOT a good Father. It's not confusing. If I allowed my daughter to be abused or gave her sickness, should I be put in jail? It is not confusing!"

Jesus is perfect divinity, and He always did and said what the Father said. He did good deeds, healing all those who came to him, raising the dead, and destroying darkness wherever He went. Satan is the one who lies, kills, and destroys. NEVER God. The Bible allows us to clarify what is clear to help us understand that which is unclear. Finally, we do not allow our pain and our questions (what we do not understand) to determine how we appreciate scripture. The Bible says that now we see dimly and only know in part, but when we graduate to heaven, everything will be revealed to us. (I Corinthians 13:12) Presently, we simply must trust in God's goodness and love. This goes right along with the section about living in the Tree of Life. Knowing that God is always good and never evil will help keep you living in the right tree.

3 Question Bible Study Work Sheet

Read God's Word

Exodus 34:6

And He passed in front of Moses, Proclaiming, "The Lord, the Lord, the compassionate and gracious God, slow to anger, abounding in love and faithfulness."

1: What Does God's Word Say? List the facts	*2:* What Does God's Word Mean? List the lessons	*3:* What Does God's Word Mean in My Life? Listen to His voice
Phrase 1 - Phrase 2 -		

Phrase 3 –		

Pray and Respond:

Write out your prayer.

Live It Out:

How will I apply this to my daily life?

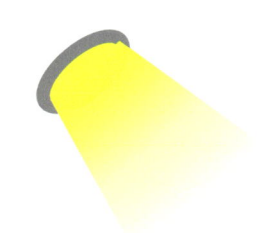

Why the Holy Spirit?

Week 3

> **Scripture of Focus: John 16:7**
>
> "But I tell you the truth, it is to your advantage that I go away; for if I do not go away, the Helper (the Holy Spirit) will not come to you; but if I go, I will send Him to you."
>
> Read pages the following pages of New Beginnings
>
> - The Holy Spirit - Page 41
> - Meditate on scripture and reading.
>
> **The Promise, Person, and Power of the Holy Spirit:**
>
> In John 16:7, Jesus told His disciples, *"It is best for you that I go away."* That does not sound smart. If we had our choice of Jesus here – physically present right here – or gone, we would choose that Jesus stay stays. What could possibly be better than having Jesus present in person? He goes on: *"But in fact, it is best for you that I go away because if I don't, the Advocate won't come. If I do go away, then I will send Him to you."* "Advocate" in Greek is "Paraclete," which means Comforter, Counselor, Encourager, and Helper. *"It is good that I go away so that He will come."* Jesus returning to heaven was for our benefit - making way for the Holy Spirit to be with us. Yet, so many Christians today do not know who He is and why it is so important to have a relationship with Him.

The book of Acts is a great place to read about the Holy Spirit. You, too, will become aware of how heavily the disciples relied on Him.

What stood out to me was the Apostle Paul and his calling upon his life. He was called first to be an apostle to the Gentiles, but because of his deep love for his Jewish countrymen. When Paul traveled to different cities to preach the Gospel, he would always first go to the Jewish synagogues.

This caused him great harm. Most of the persecution against him was from his own people, the Jews. Paul, in the beginning of his ministry, it appeared he didn't rely on the Holy Spirit like he did a few years later.

What is our takeaway from this? Holy spirit will help us stay within what God has called us to do; if you don't, like Paul, you will be asking for trouble. Another important thing to notice in the book of Acts is how much all the disciples relied on and looked to the Holy Spirit to guide them.

Acts 5:32: "We are his witnesses to these things, and so is the Holy Spirit." In the book of Acts, there are fifty-six references to the Holy Spirit.

It is very important that you understand who the Holy Spirit is. He is the most amazing, kind, wise, compassionate, and powerful person on the face of the Earth. Many people today struggle with understanding who the Holy Spirit is because they think of Him as an influence, not a person… they call Him an It. The Holy Spirit has a will, a mind, and emotions. He can be grieved. Many scriptures point to this truth. When the Holy Spirit is removed from the church, it will become a social club and a religious institution. There is no revelation or freedom without the Holy Spirit. In 2nd Corinthians, it says, "Wherever the spirit is Lord, there is freedom." Whenever the Holy Spirit is not allowed to be Lord in our churches or homes, there is no real freedom; it becomes dry, and you lose your passion for life and for Jesus.

A great saying by Bill Johnson is, 'The church that doesn't allow the Holy Spirit to have His way becomes a religion that is Form without power.'

Jesus did what He was called to do to reconcile us back to the Father. He is now with the Father, sitting on the right hand of God, interceding for us day and night as our high priest.

He sent the wonderful Holy Spirit to be with us and help us get through this tough life by constantly pointing us to Jesus. A tragic mistake many Christians make is not getting to know the work of the Holy Spirit through scriptures without first coming to know Him intimately.

Spending time with Him as a person. We need to settle it in our hearts that the Holy Spirit is a person who is infinitely wise, infinitely holy, and cares about every part of your life. If we view the Holy Spirit as just a spiritual influence from God, we will never have a deep relationship with God; it will always be shallow and lacking. And it opens us up to spiritual pride.

The Holy Spirit is part of the God Head:

Father- Jesus- and the Holy Spirit- are one (Trinity).

A good example of this is water; this one substance takes on three different forms- Ice – water – and steam. A unity of three co-eternal persons.

The Importance of the Holy Spirit:

1 Corinthians 2:10-16

Says, "These are the things God has revealed to us by His Spirit." The spirit searches all things, even the deep things of God. For who knows a person's thoughts except for their own spirit within him? In the same way, no one knows the thoughts of God except the Spirit of God. What we have received is not the spirit of the world but the spirit that is from God so that we may understand what God has freely given us. The spirit reveals the mysteries of God to us."

1. He guides you to Jesus' who is truth

Jesus was clear on the importance of the Holy Spirit: "But when He, the Spirit of truth, comes, He will guide you into all truth... He will glorify Me because it is from Me that He will receive what He will make known to you" (John 16:13-14). Do you want to know what Jesus is saying to you as you journey through this life? Do you want to be able to hear God's voice as you read through the pages of the Bible? It is the Holy Spirit, the Spirit of Truth, who communicates all of that to you. The better we get to know Him, the better we get to know Jesus.

2. He directs your steps

The Holy Spirit not only speaks the words of Jesus to you, but He is the one who leads and directs your steps into the abundant life that God desires for us. "You, however, are not in the realm of the flesh but are in the realm of the spirit, if indeed the Spirit of God lives in you. And if anyone does not have the Spirit of Christ, they do not belong to Christ. But if Christ is in you, then even though your body is subject to death because of sin, the spirit gives life[a] because of righteousness. And if the spirit of him *who raised Jesus from the dead is living in you, he who raised Christ from the dead will also give life to your mortal bodies because of[b] his spirit who lives in you." (Romans 8:9-11)*. The Holy Spirit is the conduit of life from God into your heart. He is the one who will always point you to Jesus. We must surrender our attitudes, words, and actions and follow His leadership. He will direct your steps through all the complicated paths of life and guide you away from sin. That is an abundant life!

3. He gives you spiritual gifts

The Holy Spirit is also the one who gives spiritual gifts to all followers of Jesus so that we all can walk out our destiny in the Body of Christ. Paul gave us a sampling of those gifts in his first letter to the Corinthian church: *"Now to each one the manifestation of the Spirit is given for the common good. To one, there is given through the spirit a message of wisdom, to another faith by the same spirit, to another gifts of healing by that one spirit, to another miraculous powers, to another prophecy, to another distinguishing between spirits, to another speaking in different kinds of tongues, and to still another the interpretation of tongues. All these are the work of one and the same spirit, and he distributes them to each one, just as he determines."* (1 Corinthians 12:7-11).

It is through these gifts of the spirit that we function best as the Church. It is through these gifts that we can show the power of Jesus to people who so need to know our Savior. The Bible says in Hebrews 10:24,25 to spur one another on towards love and good deeds. It isn't always easy to show love that is why the author of Hebrews gave us this challenge through the Holy Spirit, which helps us to see the best in one another. He gives us the ability to build one another up and to know how to pray for ourselves and others. Both fruit and gifts are affected by each other, but your fruit will greatly impact your gifts.

The fruit of the spirit helps you to use your gifts in a way that always glorifies God, not yourself. The fruit of the spirit must be strong in your life to use your gifts for the body.

4. HE HELPS US IN THE GROWTH PROCESS

We all love those times of encounter with God when He just wonderfully steps into our life lives and circumstances. This is amazing, but after those encounters, we have to recognize what God did. We must begin the process of making the necessary changes that lead to our transformation. **New and better attitudes and different choices.**

Sometimes, He uses an ongoing process because He wants us to know who we are and who He wants us to be for others. When we understand those dynamics, it leads us to an encounter with God through the Holy Spirit. It is the ongoing process of trust, and it is also

the process by which God takes up residence with us. In the Old Testament, God would rest upon certain individuals temporarily and give them a word. But now, because of Jesus, He inhabits us through the Holy Spirit.

We cannot escape the process, and we should not even try. It is the process that makes us rich in our relationship with God. It makes us the people of God that we are supposed to be.

Process and encounter are the way God deals with us through the Holy Spirit. He joyfully helps us grow more and more into the image of Christ. This ongoing process is a series of steps from where we are now to where God wants us to be. This empowers us to become the person God sees us in the situations that we are facing. Situations are not just about deliverance, but they are about growth, about change, and about becoming more of who we really are.

Never get discouraged about the process because if you allow the Holy Spirit to teach, you will become transformed and brought from glory to glory. Always ask the Holy Spirit what you are supposed to learn and how you can partner with Him to obtain the upgrade that God desires to give you.

5. He empowers you to be bold for the GOSPEL and to walk in power

In Acts, Luke recalls over and over the crucial role the Holy Spirit played in the early Church's proclamation of the Gospel. When Peter and John stood accused before powerful leaders, Luke reported that Peter, being filled with the Holy Spirit, boldly proclaimed that Jesus Christ of Nazareth, the One they had crucified, was the only way to salvation (Acts 4:5-12). This is the same Peter who only two months earlier had denied Jesus. Standing in the very place where Jesus had been condemned, Peter accused these religious elites of crucifying the Messiah. That new boldness could only be possible through the empowering of the Holy Spirit. The Bible states that the spirit was so strong in Peter that even his shadow healed people.

When Paul was speaking to the Corinthian church, he told them to pursue earnestly the gifts of the spirit. A couple of chapters later, Paul speaks about pursuing an encounter with the Holy Spirit. Paul said you need to pursue the anointing for the power to demonstrate the gifts of the Holy Spirit! In the Western churches, we overcomplicate things. It is the revelation that is the invitation for the encounter. This makes us able to demonstrate the reality of what God says to walk in the power of God.

When Jesus was baptized, a dove descended on Him from heaven and rested on Him. This symbolized that the Holy Spirit was now in Him, and after that day, He began to do many miracles. The Bible says that Jesus did so many miracles the world couldn't contain enough books about all of them. It is remarkable the differences in all of the disciples when they were baptized with the Holy Spirit and fire… That's what He does. He brings fire in us! Jesus said because of the Holy Spirit, we would do even greater miracles than He did. The Holy Spirit is what qualifies us for the impossible. Bill Johnson says, "One person and the Holy Spirit equals no impossibilities!" Amen!

This fire is meant to be shared with others to **Go** and tell the lost about Jesus. All believers should be evangelical Christians. Jesus commanded us **all** to share the good news with others. The Holy Spirit will help you not only with boldness, but He will give you the words you need to say to touch deep into their hearts. Start with sharing your testimony. Someone can argue theology, but they can't argue about your personal story.

Please read Romans 10:11-15, 1 Corinthians 10:31, and Mathew 28:18,19

Lastly, when we do this, we glorify God, and it is pleasing to Him.

1 Timothy 2:3-4 says, "This is good, and it is pleasing in the sight of God our Savior, who desires all people to be saved and to come to the knowledge of the truth."

I read a good Rick Warren quote once that is very thought-provoking… **"The way you store up treasure in heaven is by investing in getting people there."**

3 Question Bible Study Work Sheet

Read God's Word

John 16:7

"But I tell you the truth, it is to your advantage that I go away; for if I do not go away, the Helper (the Holy Spirit) will not come to you; but if I go, I will send Him to you."

1: What Does God's Word Say? List the facts	*2:* What Does God's Word Mean? List the lessons	*3:* What Does God's Word Mean in My Life? Listen to His voice
Phrase 1 - Phrase 2 -		

Phrase 3 –		

Pray and Respond:

Write out your prayer.

Live It Out:

How will I apply this to my daily life?

How do I follow Jesus? And how do I have a Jesus Culture?

Week 4

Scripture of Focus: I Peter 1:14

"As obedient children, do not be conformed to the passions of your former self. But as He who called you is holy, you also be holy in all your conduct."

Read the following pages of New Beginning

- Following Jesus – Page 29
- Baptism – Page 25
- Talking to God - Page 33
- Make a Plan - Page 37
- Living life with purpose - Page 47

Meditate on scripture and reading.

There are many things I could say here about what it means to be a Christ follower and to have a Jesus Culture. I know you would agree that the world is on a slippery slope. Now more than ever, we must stand out so the world can see that there is hope and that living our lives in Jesus's culture is the way to live your life with true joy.

One of the biggest areas the enemy is going after is in our families, our children, gender identity, race divisions, and the church.

I love Lisa Bevere, and I wanted to share some things she said at a conference regarding Jesus's culture.

I love Lisa Bevere, and I wanted to share some things she said at a conference regarding Jesus's culture.

She spoke about gender war causing confusion and division. Sadly, today, men are being emasculated, and women are being told they're a problem.

Too many women have the mistaken opinion that your femininity is a problem. But God says You are an answer to the problem. She shared a story during the conference that a high-ranking special Op's officer called her regarding the need for her book "Lioness Arising." He wanted every woman in his special op's team going to Afghanistan to have one. He asked Lisa if she knew why we were not winning the war there. "No," she replied.

He answered it's because we are not allowed to talk to women. When you can't talk to a woman, you cannot flip a culture, and if you cannot flip the culture, you cannot win the war.

Women, we need to walk in our God's destiny when we open our mouths. It must be with wisdom and kindness. We need to be faithful stewards of the heart of the husband, faithful stewards of the heart of our family, and faithful stewards of the heart of the church.

Women men are not your answer, and they're not your problem either. We must not buy into the anger of the men who have to pay for our past. We must understand that the enemy is trying to divide the men from the women. The black from the white and the children from the parents. God is trying to heal, and the enemy is trying to kill and destroy.

Men, women are not your answer either... or your problem. A man of God values things of heaven over the things of the flesh. He makes his relationship with God his priority. He fights for his family on his knees and tells the devil, "Not today!"

Gender was never supposed to be an issue of division. Gender is supposed to be an issue of strength. When people are broken, they will try to fix themselves on the outside. But we need to understand that we are not defined by our gender but by "whose we are." We need to be somebody who gets people into the presence of God. His presence is what heals us and where He calls us his own. We need to understand the power of being a woman and the power of being a man. We need you, men, to walk in your God-given strength.

There has been so much anger and blame in the past. This has never accomplished the righteous purposes of God.

But what some have allowed to happen is we have given our culture more influence over us than the scriptures. Our culture has said if there is going to be healing in the genders, we need the women to act like men and the men to act like women. And we can all meet in the middle somewhere. But what God is saying is, "You don't understand. There is beauty in both masculinity, and there is beauty in being feminine. I want my daughters to remember that I am the one that wove them in wonder." It is hard not to miss what is happening right now. Anyone can say they're a woman now. Do you think that's a compliment, or do you think there is something undermining the very purpose of our gender? The fact that we partner with God to bring forth life. The fact that we were created to be an answer. We must get this in our mindset that the time for you to be that answer is now! Speak up and speak the truth in love. We are not called spectators. The church, for too long, has tried to be 'tolerant'. Look where it has gotten us. As we live our lives following the Jesus culture, we must stand out and speak out.

Having a Jesus culture is also being aware of our love walk, to walk in the fruit of the spirit, not just the gifts of the spirit where you are salt and light to a dark world.

Ephesians is one of the best books of the Bible that speaks to this. It is difficult to do that if we don't first know how much we are dearly loved. I love this passage in the passion translation.

Ephesians 1:3-7 in The Passion translation:

Every spiritual blessing in the heavenly realm has already been lavished upon us as a love gift from our wonderful heavenly Father, the Father of our Lord Jesus—all because he sees us wrapped into Christ. This is why we celebrate him with all our hearts! Ephesians 1:3-6

-And in love, he chose us before he laid the foundation of the universe! Because of his great love, he ordained us so that we would be seen as holy in his eyes with an unstained innocence.

-For it was always in his perfect plan to adopt us as his delightful children, through our union with Jesus, the Anointed One, so that his tremendous love that cascades over us would

glorify his grace—for the same love he has for the Beloved, Jesus, he has for us. And this unfolding plan brings him great pleasure! "

-Since we are now joined to Christ, we have been given the treasures of redemption by his blood—the total cancellation of our sins—all because of the cascading riches of his grace.

-This superabundant grace is already powerfully working in us, releasing all forms of wisdom and practical understanding. "Amen and Amen!

Baptism is another way to have a Jesus Culture:

For 2,000 years, baptism has been the defining mark of the followers of Christ and one of the first steps of obedience to Him. Matthew 3 records that Jesus started His ministry by being baptized. In Matthew 28, Jesus challenged His followers to "*make disciples of all nations, baptizing them...*". Jesus modeled and encouraged baptism for His followers.

What exactly is baptism? Baptism is a public confession of faith. It is the moment we declare to the world who we are and, most importantly, whose we are. We declare that we, through Christ, are people who are free from our past and filled with hope for our future. Baptism is a powerful symbol of what Jesus did for us. When we go under the water, we are reminded of Jesus's death on the cross and His payment for our sins. But when we come up, we are reminded that three days later, Jesus rose from the dead. Baptism reminds us the old is gone. The new has come! Being baptized is very important, but not because it saves you. The grace of God through faith in Jesus is what saves you. Getting baptized is telling the world you have decided to follow Jesus! If you haven't yet, do it soon. **This is an important next step in your walk with God.**

Do you feel it is important to be baptized, and why?

Talking to God:

Did you know that part of the Jesus culture is that we can talk to God, and He answers us? His soft voice is always speaking to us. John 10:27: "*My sheep hear my voice, and I know them, and they follow me.*

Here are a few ways God speaks to us:

God can speak through circumstances. Remember the story about Jonah and the whale? God spoke to Jonah first with His voice, but Jonah did not heed God's voice. God spoke to Jonah through circumstances—first, being swallowed by a great fish, and second, when a vine grew up to shade Jonah, and then the vine withered. It is an interesting story. You can read about it in Jonah 1-4. We need to examine our circumstances and ask if we are hearing the Lord through these circumstances. Ask yourself two questions: What's happening in my life right now? What is the Lord telling me through these circumstances?

God speaks through peace. It states in Colossians 3:15 *that God's peace can rule in our hearts.* The word *rule* does not just mean to merely exist. It means to reign or to be a deciding factor. If we do not have peace about a decision, then it is not from the Lord. Do not move forward unless you have peace. I have heard it called "velvet peace." This is what you feel from the Holy Spirit.

God speaks through other wise counsel. This truth is shown all through the book of Proverbs. When we seek godly counsel, we can hear the voice of God. This counsel should always complement scripture. When we seek wise, godly mentors in the Lord, the goal shouldn't be that they hear God, for that can happen. Ask them during your counseling time together to prayerfully confirm that what we have heard from the Lord is correct.

God can speak to us through dreams and visions. This pattern is shown in the lives of Joseph, Solomon, Jacob, Peter, John, and Paul. God still speaks to us in this way even today. Read Acts 2:17, where Peter quotes Joel 2:28.

God can speak through our thoughts. Amos 4:13 says that God makes known His ways to us through our thoughts. In Matthew 1:19-21, while Joseph thought about things, God spoke to Him. We need to be careful here because not every thought in our minds comes from the Lord. **When we are listening for answers, make sure our thoughts line up with scripture. So, we need to judge if it is from God. Does it align with Scripture? Does it in any way contradict the character of God?**

God speaks softly, and the only way we can really hear his voice is to be aware of any distractions. Be intentional; put aside time, and put your phone away. Take some time to tell Him how grateful you are for what He has done and worship…. Take some deep breaths and just be quiet and listen. Over time, you will learn to still your mind and hear Him. Don't get discouraged. It's His greatest desire to have fellowship with you.

Relax and talk to God… Tell Him how you feel. What are you concerned about, and how grateful you are? With practice, over time, you begin to speak fluently and naturally. When you spend time with God, sharing your heart with Him and being with Him, it builds intimacy. Just like you love it when your children or spouse share their day with you, God is the same way. He cares about every detail of your life. If you get quiet, you can hear him answer you. The secret to prayer is secret prayer. Just you and the Lord talking to each other.

Have you ever felt awkward trying to pray?

Worship and praise:

I think this is a natural segway from prayer to praise. So why do we clap our hands and raise our arms anyway? It's about gratitude and surrender. And the Bible tells us to.

When you raise your hands, you are saying I surrender all for you are worthy! **Psalms 100 says it well.**

A psalm. For giving grateful praise:

"Shout for joy to the Lord, all the Earth.

Worship the Lord with gladness;

come before him with joyful songs.

Know that the Lord is God.

It is he who made us, and we are his[a];

we are his people, the sheep of his pasture.

Enter his gates with thanksgiving

and his courts with praise;

give thanks to him and praise his name.

For the Lord is good and his love endures forever;

his faithfulness continues through all generations."

Why do we worship?

When you praise God, you are taking an opportunity to speak heart-to-heart with Him. And it is a powerful way to do spiritual warfare. There are many ways we can praise God. We can praise Him in music and by how we live our lives. Both praise and worship serve the purpose of drawing into His presence. I have spoken about the importance of pursuing His presence. When you put your focus on God instead of yourself, you are reminded that He is much bigger than any problem you are currently facing. When we raise our hands, it's a sign of surrender.

I will end this with another scripture found in **Psalms 68:4-5**

"Sing to God, sing in praise of His name, extol Him who rides on the clouds; rejoice before Him - His name is the Lord."

Reading your Bible.

FAILING TO PLAN IS PLANNING TO FAIL.

We Hit What We Set: Make a Plan.

Reading your Bible daily is an important goal to have. The definition of a plan is an intention or decision about what one is going to do. Being intentional about learning the word of God is important. Being intentional with blocking out a time with God and getting into the community is very important. They both require a plan and a goal. How did Jesus accomplish as much as He did in the short time He was here on Earth? He was intentional in doing what the Father said to do and to say what the Father said. He did not allow distractions to stop Him.

Scott Lindsey from Zondervan said there was a recent study done by Bible engagement where they polled 40,000 people from ages 8-80 years old. They wanted to see how we were engaging in scripture. They discovered something. This became a profound part of their study.

When we are in scripture one day a week, this could be turning to scripture during a church service. This has a negligible effect on several key areas of your life.

Two times a week has a negligible effect. Now, three times a week, there was a heartbeat that started happening.

Now, here is the profound discovery that if we are in scripture four times a week, it literally spikes off the chart. You would expect a gradual impact on your life, but it was one, two, three.. and shooting straight up, four!

What kind of behavior is being impacted?

Feeling lonely drops 30%

Anger issues drop 32%

Bitterness and strife with marriages and other relationships drop by 40%

Alcoholism drops 57%

Feeling spiritual stagnant drops 60%

Viewing pornography drops 61%

In the same study, they included sharing your faith. It jumps to 200% because you have confidence in God. Discipling someone jumps to 230%

There was also another study done by a Nuro scientist where they were able to trace what was going on in the mind by their synapse connections. They had people reading history books, cookbooks, science books, and different novels, and people reading the bible and other religious books. The only ones that had significant positive changes in their Nuro patterns were the ones reading the bible. The bible says in Romans, do not be conformed to the pattern of this world, but be transformed by the renewing of your mind with the word. And it also says God's word will never return to you void.

It is not recommended that you try to read through the entire Bible in one sitting, and don't try to read it cover to cover—it was not written that way, and it is not necessarily meant to be read that way. There are many Bible apps that can help you, and getting into a small group helps you grow in your faith. There is a whole section in my New Beginnings book that helps you map out a plan for reading your Bible.

Why do you think having a plan to learn how to grow in Christ would be important? What do you think would be a good plan for you?

Living Your Life with Purpose:

Most of the stories in the Bible do not start with intellect, reasoning, or logic. They are based on faith, wisdom, and trust. They are grounded, most importantly, in a relationship with a supreme God. The Lord has such a deep desire to be the Lord of everything in your life. He wants you to be free to dream and to even dream of what looks impossible. Many of us, in our most difficult times, lose heart and give up on our dreams. We might even take the dream that we thought would never happen and throw it away, but before it even hits the ground, Jesus picks it up, and He's holding on to it for us.

Jesus will stop at nothing to bring us to a place of fullness without measure. We were not created for anything less.

Have you ever experienced a time when you gave up on a dream, and Jesus picked it and saved it for you? Can you imagine what that will look like?

LIVING LIFE WITH GOD-GIVEN PURPOSE:

"A difficult time can be more readily endured if we retain the conviction that our existence holds a purpose, a cause to pursue, a person to love, a goal to achieve." – ***John Maxwell***

Some people measure success by the wealth they have accumulated, the power they have attained, or the status they have achieved. Yet, even though they have reached success beyond their wildest dreams, they still have an empty feeling — something is missing from their life. In order to fill that void and be completely fulfilled in life, their soul may be searching for something more. There are many wealthy people who are, quite frankly, some of the most miserable, fearful people in the world. They are Like the fish in the grass, just trying to succeed instead of walking in their purpose, following their God-given gifts and passions. Dancing in the water free! Although everyone is different, there are common threads that bind a life with purpose. Live life with a purpose.

Live by your beliefs and values:

People who live a life of purpose have core beliefs and values that influence their decisions, shape their day-to-day actions, and determine their short- and long-term priorities. They place significant value on being a person of high integrity and earning the trust and respect of others. The result is that they live with a clear conscience and spend more time listening to the voice of the Holy Spirit than being influenced by others. When we invite God into our lives, things change our relationship with our family, and others will change as well. As we lean on God, He will transform us to be more like Him. God will equip us with gifts, tools, and wisdom to love and honor His people. Stay true to who you are and learn to dance in the rain… do not let temporary setbacks stop you. Learn God's word so you can declare victory over your dreams and goals! **Be intentional** about looking for opportunities to share Christ with others! This will keep you in an attitude of joy and remembrance of what God has done for you as you share with others.

Set priorities:

People who live a life of purpose identify those activities that really matter and intentionally set boundaries to eliminate distractions. Most of them spend much of their time and effort in those areas. Otherwise, it is too easy to drift away in the currents of life. As the author Annie Dillard said, "How we spend our days is, of course, how we spend our lives." Think about what you are thinking about. What you think about determines what you will say. What you say will determine what you do. What you do will determine what your destiny is. The Bible says as a man or woman thinks, so is He. Purpose-driven believers spend quality time with God and are intentional about what is coming out of their mouths. They spend time **with God. And ask the Holy Spirit for wisdom and guidance. The Holy Spirit is THE MOST creative and smartest person ever!**

Follow your passion:

People who live a life of purpose wake up each morning eager to face the new day. They pursue their dreams with fervor, put their heart into everything they do, and feel that they are personally making a difference. As James Dean, the actor, said, "Dream as if you'll live forever. Live as if you'll die today."

Don't let hard times stop you:

People who live a life of purpose have an inner peace that only comes from Jesus. He said in John 14: 27, "Peace I leave with you, not as the world gives. Don't let your heart be troubled, and do not be afraid because I have overcome the world."

Graham Cooke says, "Don't ask the why questions. Ask the what …. "what must I do questions." The why keeps us a victim of our circumstances. The what question is modeled throughout the Bible. God, what must I do to partner with you for the upgrade I am getting from this temporary hardship?" As the saying goes, "The real measure of your wealth is how much you'd be worth if you lost all your money."

Don't allow regret to control you. That is a strategy of the enemy to hinder and rob us of our true identity. Stay focused on what God has assigned you to do. Keep your mind on the present. God is a present and future God.

Live a life of generosity.

People who live a life of purpose make a meaningful difference in someone else's life. They do things for others without expectation of personal gain and serve as Godly role models. They gain as much satisfaction from witnessing the success of others as witnessing their own success. A great quote by Mother Teresa says, "At the end of our life, we will not be judged by how many diplomas we have received, how much money we have made, how many great things we have done." We will be judged by how we loved, by, 'I was hungry, and you fed me, I was naked, and you clothed me. I was homeless, and you took me in.'

It can be overwhelming because there is so much need everywhere. Simplify it… Do not worry about the numbers. Just love the one in front of you.

We can feel like what we are doing is just a drop in the ocean. But the ocean would be less because of that missing drop. I can do things you cannot do. You can do things I cannot. Together, we can do great things.

The great motivator John Maxwell says, "Your attitude is a choice, and you need to have a great attitude because it gives you possibilities. Everybody has at least a few areas in their thinking and some attitudes that need to change. If you want to improve your life, you need to go after those areas."

3 Question Bible Study Work Sheet

Read God's Word

I Peter 1:14

"As obedient children, do not be conformed to the passions of your former self. But as he who called you is holy, you also be holy in all your conduct."

1: What Does God's Word Say? List the facts	*2:* What Does God's Word Mean? List the lessons	*3:* What Does God's Word Mean in My Life? Listen to His voice
Phrase 1 - Phrase 2 -		

Phrase 3 –		

Pray and Respond:

Write out your prayer.

Live It Out:

How will I apply this to my daily life?

Who is the church?

Week 5

Scripture of Focus: Romans 14:19

"So, then we pursue the things which make for peace and the building up of one another."

Read pages the following pages of New Beginning

- Doing life together… being the church - Page 21
- Join a group - Page 27
- Discovering Your Unique Design - Page 49

Meditate on scripture and reading.

Doing life together…. being the church

Giant Sequoias tower over the national parks of California – Sequoias are huge trees that rise high above the forest floor and above every other tree that grows around them. While they can reach 300 feet tall, their root systems are very shallow. Most of them are only about 12 feet deep, and they can thrive in as little as three feet of soil. Their strength is not found in the depth of their roots but in their interdependence. Their roots intertwine with one another, and they share resources. No Sequoia grows alone. They require healthy firs, cedars, and pines nearby to provide them with water and protection from erosion. Without an incredibly complex system of interdependence, the giant sequoias would not make it.

Likewise, God created us to support, encourage, and rely on one another. We need each other.

What would it look like to you to have your roots intertwined with one another? Do you have a hard time being interdependent?

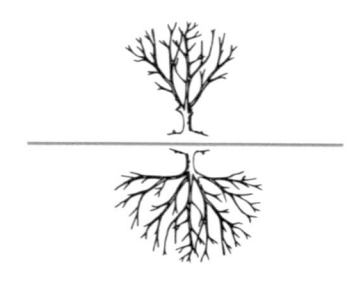

As we align our hearts with God, we make the declaration that we have His presence with us wherever we go. God is looking for bold partners to represent Him on the planet that He made for His glory. His desire is for His Kingdom to come on Earth as it is in heaven.

Kingdom of God come, the will of God be done as it is in heaven!

The Lord answers every prayer that we pray, except for those that violate His purpose. He designed us to be in fellowship with Him, to align our hearts with His heart, and to bring about His invasion!

Do you feel that something you may have requested in prayer was not consistent with God's purpose? How did that turn out?

Like Jonah and the whale, Jonah was a reluctant ambassador. The Ninevites were great enemies of Jonah's people. He did not want to be obedient when God called him to witness to the Ninevites. He would rather curse them. Jonah ran from God because he knew what God was calling him to do as a prophet of God, and Jonah did not want to do it.

Have you ever found yourself running from the will of God? How did that turn out?

Join a Group

Life is better together. Every person needs a tribe, a team, a group. Andy Stanley said, "Your friends will determine the quality and direction of your life." In John 17, Jesus prayed, "*I am praying not only for these disciples but also for all who will ever believe in me through their message. I pray that they will all be one, just as you and I are one — as you are in me, Father, and I am in you. And they may be in us so that the world will believe you sent me.*" Throughout the New Testament, we see the commands that God has called us to keep, but we cannot do it outside the context of community. We all need a support system. That support system is called a small group. God wired us for the community. The very first thing God said when He made a human, it's not good to be alone. We need each other. It's better to study the Bible together to share your life stories, to have a place to be transparent, to hear other God's stories, and to be encouraged to keep going. Small groups practice how to love. "*The disciples were devoted... to fellowship... all the believers kept meeting together, and they shared everything with each other.* "Acts 2:42-44

Why do you think being part of a group is important in the church?

Discovering Your Unique Design

You are God's masterpiece. There has never been and never will be anyone like you. That is not a testament to you; it's a testament to the God who created you. Your uniqueness is God's gift to you. What you do with that uniqueness is your gift back to God. Maturity does not equal conformity. You owe it to yourself to be yourself. But more importantly, you owe it to the One who designed you and has a destiny for you.

You are destined to do something only you can do. 1 Corinthians 12 lists various gifts given to the followers of Jesus and the different parts of the body of Christ that we, as believers, represent. The more we learn about God, the more we learn about ourselves. The more we understand the story of God, the more we understand the story we were created to live. "What comes into our minds when we think about God is the most important thing about us," is a famous quote by A.W. Tozer. It starts with, 'What is your passion'? Pay attention to what makes you excited. Teaching, speaking, organizing, etc. The Holy Spirit gives every one of us special gifts.

What do you think are your giftings?

What do you see yourself doing with these gifts? How do you think God might use your gifts for His ministry?

Doing Life Together – Being the Church

We live in a day when finding authenticity, the real thing, is more and more of a challenge. So many things are now generic or imitation. Add on the deception that is more often the rule than the exception. It is easy to become cynical in this world. This should not be the case with the church. Unfortunately, the church has been influenced by the world more than the world has been influenced by the church. If we were brutally honest, we would have to admit there are too many "superficial" or "imitation" Christians who think, talk, and live the same as their lost neighbor and co-workers.

What is a Biblical church?

"For where two or three are gathered in my name, there am I among them" (Mathew 18:20). The church consists of believers coming together in the same physical space and in the name of Jesus. To gather in the name of Jesus means to publicly worship Jesus, serve Jesus, and help others to know Jesus. Okay, we get that, but what is the church supposed to look like?

The great Apostle Paul in Ephesians wrote to the Corinthians a description of what the church should represent. The book of Ephesians is considered one of the most contemporary books in the Bible. It could have been written to the modern church. It is about us. It describes human beings, our true situation, sin, and delusion. It also describes God reaching out to people to re-create and transform them into new people. Most of the letter is about two subjects: power and identity. It describes the power of God's Spirit, which gives us the ability to have a life full of **purpose, power, and joy**, both individually and corporately with Christ.

The church is supposed to have answers to certain questions that the world desperately needs. The Western church, in many ways, has lost both its direction and its voice. The lives of Christians are too often no different than the lives of non-Christians. The Gospel, in many places, has become diluted and ineffective. We need nothing less than a new Reformation. Conversion is a renewal of the mind and transition from darkness into His marvelous light!

The church needs to recover its identity as a corporate representation of people being joined together in Christ. One of the largest failures of the church is in worship, prayer, evangelism, and discipleship.

A great quote from Bill Johnson is, "Many churches camp around the message instead of the presence. We have got to stay hungry for His presence!"

In the first book of Corinthians, Paul also identified a critical loss in the church of Corinth… they had lost their first love. Sure, they were "doing things"- using their gifts for God - but what about loving one another? Jesus said on numerous occasions that the laws of the prophets were summed up in one thing. **LOVE ONE ANOTHER!**

There is a story about a little girl who was invited to dinner at the home of her friend. The vegetable that night was buttered Brussels sprouts, and the mother asked if the little girl liked them. "Oh, yes," the child answered politely, "I *love* it!"

But when the bowl was passed, she declined to take any. The hostess said, "I thought you said you loved Brussels sprouts?" The girl replied sweetly, "Oh, yes, ma'am, I do, but not enough to *eat* them!"

Do you love your family? *"Of course I do!"* We all would say that! It is the only right answer. But what do you mean by love? So often, we love our family like that little girl loved Brussels sprouts! We love the abstract, but when it comes right down to it, we don't want to get too close. In the words of the Apostle John, we love in word, but not in deed and truth. (1 John 3:8)

What does it look like to love the way God asks us to love? We know that our relationships in our family need to be marked by love. Husbands, especially, the Bible says, are to love their wives. Wives, too, must love and respect their husbands. Parents and children, brothers and sisters are family, but just as important in the church, we must love one another, too. How do we know what such love looks like in everyday life? Paul's famous chapter on love,1 Corinthians 13, tells us.

The Corinthian church emphasized good things, spiritual gifts, to the neglect of the best. They were using their gifts apart from love. Paul makes the point that the use of their God-given gifts would amount to nothing if the Corinthians did not make love their priority.

Selfless love is the priority for every Christian.

These verses are the most profound words ever written about love. In verses 1-3, Paul's definition surpasses all others about love. He states that love is greater than all spiritual gifts because, without love, gifts are empty. In verses 4-7, he shows the *practice* of love and how love, because of its selfless characteristics, is the greatest gift. In verses 8-13, he shows the *superiority* of love and that love is greater than all spiritual gifts because it outlasts them. In our study, we are going to focus on verses 4-7, where Paul describes how love acts. Love is not talk; it is action.

We are all prone to apply verses like these to others: "My mate could sure use a lesson in love. But for me? I'm basically a loving person. I'm really easy to get along with." Forget about everybody else and ask God to apply these verses to you.

Paul defines fifteen characteristics of love to show how love acts and what love looks like in everyday life. A New Testament definition of *agape* is *"a caring, self-sacrificing commitment which shows itself in seeking the highest good of the one loved."* Jesus Christ, in His sacrificial death on the cross, is the epitome and embodiment of this kind of love. A whole series of sermons could easily be preached on these qualities of love, but it is important to spend a little time with each of them.

1. Selfless love is patient

Ouch! Why did he put that first? Patience is an interesting quality in that when we do not need it, we want it. It is when things start to irritate or frustrate us that we need patience, but usually, at that point, we do not want to be patient! Can you relate?

The Greek word comes from two words meaning "long tempered." If you're patient, you are slow to anger, and you endure personal wrongs without retaliating. You accept others' imperfections, faults, and differences. You give them time to change or room to make mistakes without coming down hard on them. Do you do that, men, with your wife and children? How about you wives?

2. Selfless love is kind

Kindness is patience in action. The Greek word comes from a word meaning "useful." A kind person is disposed to being helpful. He seeks out needs and looks for opportunities to meet those needs without repayment. He is tender and forgiving when wronged. The word patience was used in mellow wine and suggests a person who is gentle, who has the ability to soothe hurt feelings, to calm an upset person, and to help quietly in practical ways.

The kind person shows kindness in response to harsh treatment. Jesus said, *"And if you do good to those who do good to you, what credit is that to you? For even sinners do the same thing... But love your enemies, and do good, and lend, expecting nothing in return; and your reward will be great, and you will be sons of the Highest; for He Himself is kind to ungrateful and evil men"* (Luke 6:33-35). The kindness of God leads us to repentance (Romans 2:4). Kindness motivates others toward positive change.

As with patience, the real proving ground for kindness is the home. If you're patient, you are slow to anger, and you endure personal wrongs without retaliating. Arise Life describes this as 'calling out the gold in one another.' Do you, do we do that with one another?

3. Selfless love is not jealous

The word jealousy means to eagerly desire. It is used both positively and negatively in the Bible. Jealousy, in the negative sense, is related to greed and selfishness. The jealous person wants what others have; he wants things for himself. He is too selfish to applaud others' success; he must have all the attention. He wants it all for himself. James says that jealousy is often the source of quarrels and conflicts (James 4:2).

4. & 5. Selfless love does not brag and is not arrogant.

These ugly twins are related. They both stem from selfishness and are the flip side of jealousy. Jealousy is wanting what someone else has. Bragging is trying to make others jealous of what we have. Jealousy puts others down; bragging builds us up.

Bragging is an outward manifestation of pride.

The bragging person tries to impress others with his or her accomplishments in order to make himself look good: "After all I've done for you, and you treat me this way!" But love isn't trying to build oneself up; love is trying to build up the other person. Love is humble. The humble, loving person is aware that everything he has is an undeserved gift from God (1 Cor.4:7). He does not boast but thankfully uses what God has given him to serve others.

So why focus so much on Love? It is like the main verse in an early charismatic song. 'And they will know we are Christians by our love.' That is the core of "Being" the church. That is who we are. We love one another. The Apostle John wrote beautifully that God is love, and those who know God love because God is love. How can we say we love God, whom we don't see when we do not love our brothers and sisters who we do see? That is how we will become this beautiful diamond shining brightly against the darkness.

3 Question Bible Study Work Sheet

Read God's Word

Romans 14:19

"So, then we pursue the things which make for peace and the building up of one another."

1: What Does God's Word Say? List the facts	*2:* What Does God's Word Mean? List the lessons	*3:* What Does God's Word Mean in My Life? Listen to His voice
Phrase 1 - Phrase 2 -		

Phrase 3 –		

Pray and Respond:

Write out your prayer.

Live It Out:

How will I apply this to my daily life?

I bless everyone who reads this study guide to first know how deep God's love is for them so that they can truly love others well. We want to be purposeful and to stir one another toward good deeds and love. Through the help of the Holy Spirit, you can walk in your truest identity and power as sons and daughters of the one true God who is for you always and forever. Amen.

Terri Leonard